THE BOX JELLYFISH

BY COLLEEN SEXTON

BELLWETHER MEDIA • MINNEAPOLIS, MN

Jump into the cockpit and take flight with Pilot Books. Your journey will take you on high-energy adventures as you learn about all that is wild, weird, fascinating, and fun!

This edition first published in 2012 by Bellwether Media, Inc.

No part of this publication may be reproduced in whole or in part without written permission of the publisher. For information regarding permission, write to Bellwether Media, Inc., Attention: Permissions Department, 5357 Penn Avenue South, Minneapolis, MN 55419.

Library of Congress Cataloging-in-Publication Data

Sexton, Colleen A., 1967-
  The box jellyfish / by Colleen Sexton.
     p. cm. – (Pilot books. Nature's deadliest)
  Includes bibliographical references and index.
  Summary: "Fascinating images accompany information about the box jellyfish. The combination of high-interest subject matter and narrative text is intended for students in grades 3 through 7"–Provided by publisher.
  ISBN 978-1-60014-664-0 (hardcover : alk. paper)
  1. Cubomedusae–Juvenile literature. I. Title.
  QL377.S4S46 2011
  593.5'3–dc23   2011017708

Printed in the United States of America, North Mankato, MN.

080111   1187

CONTENTS

A Dangerous Swim _____ 4

Tentacles, Stinging Cells,
   and Venom _____ 8

Preventing Stings _____ 18

Glossary _____ 22

To Learn More _____ 23

Index _____ 24

A Dangerous Swim

On a summer day in northeastern Australia, 10-year-old Rachael Shardlow went for a swim in the Calliope River. As she was splashing in the water with her older brother, Sam, Rachael felt something wrap around her legs. She was tangled in the **tentacles** of a box jellyfish! The jellyfish tightened its tentacles around Rachael, stinging her and injecting deadly **venom** into her body.

Seconds later, Rachael told her brother that she couldn't see or breathe. Sam pulled her away from the jellyfish, ripping some of the tentacles. He carried her to their parents on the riverbank. Rachael asked her family if she was going to die, and then she passed out.

5

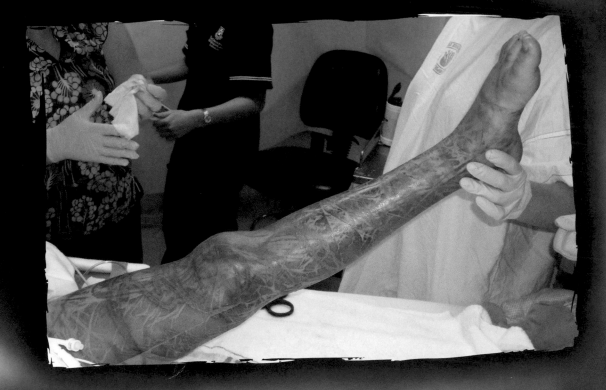

Pieces of the box jellyfish's tentacles still clung to Rachael's legs. A couple camping nearby knew to pour **vinegar** on the tentacles to prevent more stings. Because she had passed out, Rachael didn't feel the tremendous pain that jellyfish venom causes. Rachael's parents rushed her to the hospital. On the way, she stopped breathing and turned blue. Rachael's father performed **CPR** to keep her breathing.

Two days later, Rachael woke up in the hospital. She stayed there for six weeks recovering. By that time, her injuries were no longer painful. Rachael went home with scars on her legs and some short-term memory loss, but she had survived.

Victims usually survive minor stings from box jellyfish. Experts say that Rachael is the only person to survive such serious stings. The jellyfish's venom quickly attacks the heart, **nervous system**, and muscles. It can kill in less than four minutes, often before the victim can be rescued from the water. A person who is badly stung rarely survives. Rachael is lucky to be alive. People call her survival a miracle.

Accidental Stings

Box jellyfish are predators that sting and eat other animals for food. They do not prey on humans. They only sting people who accidentally swim too close.

After the Attack

Today, Rachael's wounds are still healing. She enjoys playing netball and soccer and is beginning to learn tennis. Though Rachael often swims at Lake Awoonga, she stays out of saltwater to avoid another encounter with the box jellyfish!

Tentacles, Stinging Cells, and Venom

The box jellyfish is the most feared of all jellyfish. Its powerful venom makes it one of the world's deadliest creatures. Box jellyfish live in the warm ocean waters north of Australia. They are found as far north as the Philippines. They float in calm, shallow waters near shore, especially where rivers meet the ocean. These are also popular places for people to swim.

The Philippines

Australia

box jellyfish territory = ☐

A Taste for Tentacles

Large sea turtles prey on box jellyfish. Scientists don't know how the turtles can swallow the jellyfish without getting stung. It may be that their shells and thick skin protect them from the venom.

Unrivaled Venom

There are over 30 known species of box jellyfish. The smallest species is the size of a jelly bean. While a few species can cause death in humans, the sea wasp is by far the most dangerous of all box jellyfish.

Box jellyfish have pale blue bodies. Swimmers often have trouble seeing the deadly creatures because they blend in with the water. Their **transparency** acts as **camouflage**, protecting them from predators. It also helps box jellyfish surprise prey. Fish that swim into a jellyfish's tentacles quickly become food. While most jellyfish drift with ocean currents, box jellyfish often chase their prey. They can reach a speed of 5 miles (8 kilometers) per hour.

The box jellyfish gets its name from the boxy shape of its **bell**. The soft, smooth bell can grow to be the size of a basketball. The jellyfish does not have a head, a heart, ears, bones, blood, or legs. Its mouth is in the center of its body. Instead of a brain, the box jellyfish has a **nerve net** that senses changes in light or direction. The jellyfish has 24 eyes that are arranged in groups of six. Two eyes in each group work like human eyes. However, scientists have yet to discover how box jellyfish can process what they see without a brain.

Made of Water

About 95 percent of a box jellyfish's body is water. If one is taken out of the sea, it becomes very flat and squishy.

Stringy tentacles that measure up to 10 feet (3 meters) long hang from a box jellyfish's body. As many as 15 tentacles grow from each corner of the bell. They tangle together to form a net that traps anything that swims near.

The box jellyfish uses **stinging cells** to defend itself and kill prey. Thousands of stinging cells cover each tentacle. Each cell contains a tiny stinger shaped like a dart. The cells fire these darts when the tentacle comes in contact with chemicals on the victim's skin. With the brush of a single tentacle, thousands of stinging cells fire powerful venom into a victim. As the victim struggles to get away, the tentacle clings tighter and more stinging cells are triggered.

The venom of a sea wasp
is so powerful that about
1 ounce (30 milliliters)
can kill 60 adult humans!

16

Most chance meetings with box jellyfish involve minor, treatable stings. Some encounters, however, can result in thousands of stings and a deadly amount of venom entering the victim's body. The powerful venom starts to work right away. First, a victim feels the pain of the sting itself. Some victims die of heart failure within minutes or go into shock because of the intense pain. Venom affects victims so quickly that they often drown before they are able to swim to shore. Survivors are left with white marks on their skin. Later, these whip-like marks turn red, blister, and scar.

Preventing Stings

The best way to avoid a box jellyfish sting is to stay out of the waters in which they live. Signs posted at beaches and along rivers warn people of the danger. Some beaches protect swimmers by putting up nets that keep box jellyfish out. Swimmers, snorkelers, and scuba divers often wear stinger suits. These lightweight suits cover the entire body to keep the skin's chemicals from triggering a jellyfish's stinging cells.

Someone who is stung by a box jellyfish needs immediate medical attention. Help the victim out of the water and get a lifeguard or call an emergency number. The victim may need CPR if the venom has affected his or her breathing or caused heart failure. It's also important to prevent more venom from entering the victim's system. Pouring vinegar over the remaining tentacles will prevent the stinging cells from firing. They should be carefully washed away with saltwater or removed with gloved hands. A tool, such as a stick, shell, or tweezers, could also be used. The victim should then be taken to a hospital as quickly as possible.

In recent years, the population of box jellyfish has been on the rise. The number of reported stings has also increased. Experts believe overfishing of the ocean has driven jellyfish closer to shore to find prey.

In the coming years, **climate change** may also affect the population of box jellyfish. These sea animals are used to living in warm, tropical waters. Some scientists believe that as the temperature of ocean water rises, the box jellyfish's territory could start spreading northward. Experts worry that if the box jellyfish moves into new coastal areas, more people could become victims of its deadly sting.

Attack Facts

- In Australia, box jellyfish stings have killed 68 people since 1883.
- In the Philippines, 20 to 40 people die every year from box jellyfish stings.

bell—the body of a jellyfish

camouflage—coloring and markings that hide an animal by making it look like its surroundings

climate change—any long-term weather change in an area

CPR—an emergency medical procedure performed on someone whose heart and lungs have stopped working; CPR stands for cardiopulmonary resuscitation.

nerve net—a network of nerves without a brain; a jellyfish's nerve net allows it to respond to changes in its environment.

nervous system—a system of the body; the brain, spinal cord, and nerves make up the nervous system.

stinging cells—cells on a jellyfish's tentacles that push stingers into fish or other prey; stingers shoot venom into prey.

tentacles—thin, flexible extensions that some sea creatures use to capture prey

transparency—the quality of being clear or see-through

venom—a poison that some animals make; a few species of box jellyfish produce deadly venom.

vinegar—a sour liquid used to flavor and preserve food; vinegar contains acid that helps treat jellyfish stings.

To Learn More

At the Library

Cheshire, Gerard. *Jellyfish*. New York, N.Y.:
Franklin Watts, 2008.

Gross, Miriam J. *The Jellyfish*. New York, N.Y.: Rosen Pub.
Group's PowerKids Press, 2006.

Lunis, Natalie. *Box Jellyfish: Killer Tentacles*. New York, N.Y.:
Bearport Pub., 2010.

On the Web

Learning more about box jellyfish
is as easy as 1, 2, 3.

1. Go to www.factsurfer.com.

2. Enter "box jellyfish" into the search box.

3. Click the "Surf" button and you will see a list of
related Web sites.

With factsurfer.com, finding more information
is just a click away.

Index

attack facts, 21
attacks, 7, 21
Australia, 4, 8, 21
bell, 12, 14
body, 11, 12, 13, 14
Calliope River, 4
camouflage, 11
climate change, 21
CPR, 6, 18
heart failure, 7, 17, 18
nerve net, 12
pain, 6, 17
Philippines, 8, 21
predators, 7, 11
prey, 11, 15, 21
scars, 6, 17
sea wasp, 10, 16
Shardlow, Rachael, 4, 6, 7
Shardlow, Sam, 4
stinger suits, 18

stinging, 4, 7, 9, 15, 16, 17,
    18, 21
stinging cells, 15, 18
swimming, 4, 7, 8, 11, 14,
    17, 18
tentacles, 4, 6, 9, 11, 14,
    15, 18
territory, 8, 21
transparency, 11
venom, 4, 6, 7, 8, 9, 10, 15,
    16, 17, 18
vinegar, 6, 18

The images in this book are reproduced through the courtesy of: Roger Steene/
imagequestmarine.com, front cover, pp. 12-13; Juan Martinez, pp. 4-5; Geoff Shardlow, pp. 6,
7; Jurgen Freund/naturepl.com, pp. 8-9; Rich Carey, pp. 10-11; Paul Sutherland/Getty Images,
pp. 14-15, 18-19; Dr. David Wachenfeld/Minden Pictures, pp. 16-17; Seth Resnick/Getty
Images, p. 17; OceanwideImages.com, pp. 20-21.